Stories from the Bible

First published in Great Britain and in the USA in 2016 by Frances Lincoln Children's Books,
74-77 White Lion Street, London N1 9PF, UK
QuartoKnows.com
Visit our blogs at QuartoKnows.com

A CIP catalogue record for this book is available from the British Library.

ISBN 978-1-84780-833-2

Illustrated in gouache

Edited by Katie Cotton • Designed by Nicola Price
Commissioned by Rachel Williams • Production by Laura Grandi

Printed in China
10 9 8 7 6 5 4 3 2

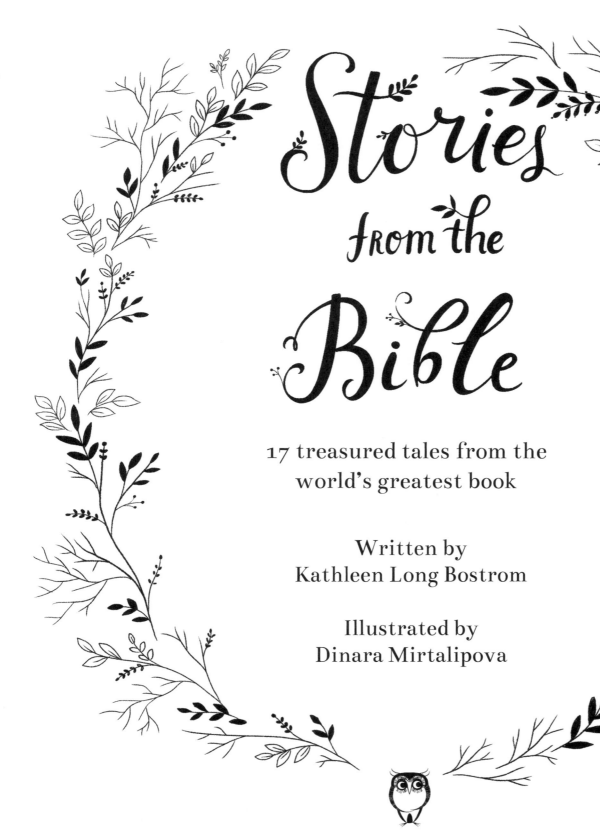

Stories from the Bible

17 treasured tales from the
world's greatest book

Written by
Kathleen Long Bostrom

Illustrated by
Dinara Mirtalipova

Frances Lincoln
Children's Books

With love to Carrie, Stefano, Matteo, and Francesca.
You are always in our hearts.
Swear-Bear-Mer forever!
Love,
K. L. B.

To my beloved grandma Lilia Sergeyevna Talipova (Charbadze)
1927—2008
D. M.

Contents

The Old Testament

The Creation

Every story has a beginning.

The story of creation begins with God. He was there before anything else.

God can do anything, and has the most amazing imagination ever. So right at the beginning, where our story starts, God decided to create.

Imagine a blank page, with no words or pictures, or a song without music or lyrics. That's how it was, before God made the heavens and the earth.

There were no trees, or mountains, or birds, or animals, or people. Just swirling, deep waters, shapeless, dark and empty.

Nothingness.

The Spirit of God – God's breath – hovered over these waters.

God thought, brooded, mused and contemplated. "What shall I do with all this nothingness?" Then his imagination took flight.

God decided to create with words.

"Light!" God said, and liked the sound of that. "Let there be light!"

And just like that, came light.

God said, "It's good, the light."

God untangled the light from the dark, one from another, then gave the light and the dark names.

"Light, I shall call 'day'. And dark, I shall call 'night'."

Now that day and night had come, the first whole day happened.

Along with light, and with day and night, God created seconds and minutes and hours, which had never been before. Time began.

But God's imagination didn't stop there.

"Something must be done with all this water," God thought. Gushing, and rushing, the waters flowed everywhere.

God pushed some of the water up, and created the sky, with all its many moods.

"That's good! Sky."

Another evening and morning had passed, Day Two.

The water on the earth covered everything. God thought, brooded, mused and contemplated. "Ah!" God said. "Land! And sea!" And he gathered the water into crashing, splashing oceans and seas, and shimmering, glimmering lakes that trickled and rippled into streams and creeks and puddles. Land spilled out and settled beneath the sky, mighty mountains and valleys, rocks and sand and clay.

"Good," God said.

But Day Three was not over yet. God danced, and the land shimmied and shook, and up from the ground arose plants and trees of every kind you can imagine, and more. The trees and plants clapped their hands in praise:

beech, bottlebrush and baobab;

cactus, carob and coconut;

ginkgo, gum and guava;

maple, mahogany and mango;

palm, pawpaw and poplar, to name just a few.

On the trees and plants, seeds and fruits and vegetables burst forth:

cantaloupe and kumquats;

broccoli and bamboo;

potatoes and peanuts.

And the flowers, oh, the flowers! Hibiscus, iris, lotus, orchid, rose, tulip – an entire alphabet of flowers, each one soaked with colour.

Colour! Suddenly, the world filled with colours; not just red, orange, yellow, green, blue and purple, but vermilion, ochre, maize, emerald, periwinkle, heliotrope, magenta, sepia, ebony, cream. God wrapped the world in ribbons of rainbows.

Smells, lovely scents that hadn't existed before now filled the air:

sweet jasmine, spicy lilac, pungent pine.

God breathed in and out and the flowers waved in the breeze.

What a dazzling day of wonders, Day Three! "Good, good, good!" God said.

On Day Four, God gazed across the sky, gathered up a big batch of light and formed it into shape. This fiery ball, God named 'sun'.

God fiddled around with rocks and dust and came up with 'moon'. The moon reflects the sun, so both day and night shine with their own, special lights.

The sun and moon marked time into days and weeks, and seasons: summer, autumn, winter, spring, each with its own wonders.

God clapped with joy and sent sparkling stars throughout the whole universe, to glimmer and glisten and gleam. The beauty of the heavens sang their Creator's glory.

"Good," said God.

On Day Five, God went beyond colours and smells, and created noise.

Well, what he really created were water creatures and birds.

From whales to whelks,

urchins to octopuses,

sharks to starfish to sea horses,

God made creatures of the water.

From bobolinks to buffleheads,

kookaburras to crows,

pelicans to peacocks,

God made birds of the air.

And oh, the noise! Splishing, splashing fins! Fluttering, flapping wings! Shrieks and squawks, hooting, howling, joyful sounds crowded the sea and sky.

"Fill the world!" God laughed. "Fill the world with life and noise!"

With the sea and sky full, God began Day Six by constructing the creatures of the land. More colours! More smells! More noise! The Creator's imagination could not be stopped.

Romping, stomping, hurrying, scurrying, rip-roaring creatures crawled and climbed and cavorted everywhere.

Great, gangly giraffes. Enormous-eared elephants. Slithering snakes. Awesome ocelots. On and on, God kept creating creatures.

God painted patterns on the creatures of the sea and sky and land.

Zigzag zebras, dotted Dalmatians, colourful chameleons.

Somewhere in the midst of all this, God made bugs and butterflies and all the creeping, crawling, buzzing, busy creatures, and blessed them all, each and every one.

God loved the green pastures, the still waters, the majestic mountains, and all the living things. God loved the colours and smells and sounds. God loved it all.

"Good, good, good!" he said.

But the best part of creation came last.

God needed someone to take care of the earth, the sea and sky, the grass and mountains, and all the trees, plants, flowers, birds and creatures.

Think, think, think. God thought, brooded, mused, and contemplated.

And this all-powerful God with the amazing imagination said, "That's it! My final creation will be people! They will be a reflection of me, able to think, love and create, to know right from wrong, to be kind-hearted and caring. They will treasure this beautiful world and will be glad to share it with one another. I will love them, and they will love me, and they will take care of all that I have made."

God took the dust from the earth and created Adam, whose name means 'from the earth'. And so Adam would not be alone, God then created Eve, whose name means 'life'. God breathed God's breath – God's Spirit – into the man, Adam, and the woman, Eve, and set them down in the world, to live in peace and harmony

among the wonders of creation.

"This is not just good, it's very good! Excellent!" God said.

Perfect.

For the very first time since the beginning, God spoke directly to creation. "Look around!" he said to Adam and Eve. "Look at this beautiful world. I give it all to you – everything! Take good care of the heavens and the earth, the sky and the land and the sea, the trees and the plants and the flowers, the sun and the moon and the stars, the fish and the birds and all the living creatures."

Adam and Eve sang praises. They loved each other, and they loved God. Everything was just as it was meant to be.

God smiled at the heavens and the earth, took a deep breath, and decided to sit back and enjoy it all. So on Day Seven, now that everything was in place, the Creator of everything rested. That day was declared to be a special day, a holy day, a day to give thanks and to remember that once, long ago, the story began.

The Garden of Eden

Now, in this wonderful world, there was a garden overflowing with lush trees plump with ripe, juicy fruit. Colourful birds rested in the branches of the trees, chattering and chirping and filling the garden with cheerful sounds.

Clear, cool water babbled and giggled over rocks and ran in silvery streams and rivers and watered the trees and grass.

God named the garden, 'Eden', which means 'pleasure' and 'delight', and indeed, the Garden of Eden was just such a place.

Adam and Eve lived in that garden.

God gave them everything they needed: a safe place to be with all the food they could want. They were never lonely, and never afraid. God loved them. They trusted their Creator.

One thing, and one thing only, they were told to leave alone.

"Eat from all the trees you want," God said to them. "Except the one in the middle of the garden, the tree of the knowledge of good and evil."

Adam and Eve didn't think any more about that tree. They didn't need anything other than what they already had.

But one day, a snake made them think twice. This snake was sly, sneaky and eager to trick Adam and Eve into doing something to displease God.

"That tree in the middle of the garden?" The snake hissed at Eve. "Why shouldn't you have that fruit? It will make you wise, like God. Eating it won't hurt anything. Trust me."

Eve knew better, but the snake made her doubt what God had said about that one tree.

It looked more beautiful than all the other trees and the fruit looked tastier than anything else in the garden. Eve reached out her hand, and before she could stop herself, she plucked a fruit from its branches and took a bite. And because she shared everything with Adam, she gave him a bite, too.

And right away, Adam and Eve knew that they had done something wrong. They'd never done anything wrong before, and it did not feel good. It made them afraid.

God liked to talk with Adam and Eve, and they enjoyed talking with him. But that evening, when God came to the garden to visit, they hid.

"Adam! Eve!" God called. "Where are you?"

God knew immediately what Adam and Eve had done. They had never hidden from him before.

"What have you done?" God asked them. "Did you eat from the tree, the one from which I told you not to eat? Why would you do that?"

Adam and Eve blamed each other. They'd never done that before, either. They never had a reason to, before they decided to turn away from God.

God felt more sad than ever before. Sad, angry and disappointed.

God knew that things would never be the same.

The fruit fell from the trees, *drop, plop, squish*! The birds stopped chattering and chirping. The water ran like tears in the rivers.

God told the snake, "Get out of my sight! Because of what you have done, from now on, you will crawl on the ground, in the dust, and all will be afraid of you."

God turned to Adam and Eve. "You must leave this garden," he said in a sad voice. "I gave you everything you needed. I gave you this world, and each other. I promised to take care of you. But you did not trust me. You don't belong here any more."

Before Adam and Eve left the garden, God stitched up clothes for them, then he sent them on their way.

Everything had changed.

Except for one thing: God still loved Adam and Eve, more than they knew.

Nothing could ever change that.

Noah and the Ark

Once God had created time, it began to pass. Seconds, minutes, hours, days, weeks, and seasons: summer, autumn, winter, spring.

After many years had passed, people forgot about God.

They forgot how much God loved them and they forgot that their Creator had asked them to take care of all living things.

People became violent. Mean. Selfish. They no longer praised God. They only wanted things for themselves, no matter how much it hurt others, no matter how much it hurt the world.

God got angry. He had not created the plants and trees and all the amazing creatures to be treated this way. God had not created people to be cruel. As he saw what people were doing to one another and to creation, God got angry, but he was also sad. Very, very sad.

In fact, God's heart broke.

"I will start over," God thought. "I will get rid of all creation, and begin again."

But the Creator could not quite give up on everything and everyone. There was one man, Noah, who still loved God. Noah raised his three sons to love God, too, and to take care of all the living creatures. When the rest of the world turned away from God, Noah did not.

And because there was still a flicker of love and kindness in the world, God decided to save it.

"Build a boat," he said to Noah. "Build it with enough room for you and your wife, your sons and their wives. Build it with enough room for all the different kinds of animals and birds. And don't forget the food! You're going to need enough to feed everyone for a long, long time. There's a big flood coming."

Noah did exactly as God asked. He built a huge boat, called an ark, with rooms for his family. He built decks, stalls, pens, coops, nests and cages for all the creatures: the pelicans, peacocks and penguins; the gangly giraffes, enormous-eared elephants and awesome ocelots.

It took a long time to build the ark, but Noah did not give up, for God had not given up on him.

As God commanded, Noah made sure to have males and females of all the creatures, and plenty of food. Once it was finished, Noah loaded everyone and everything onto the ark.

And then it began to rain.

It rained and rained and rained. It rained for forty days and forty nights. The puddles turned to vast lakes and the lakes to seas and soon the ark was afloat on top of the deep water, with no land in sight.

The never-ending rain, the absence of land, the angry sky crashing with lightning and thunder, all of this frightened the animals. Shrieking, squawking, hooting and howling birds, and romping, stomping, hurrying, scurrying, rip-roaring creatures shuddered and shivered on the decks and in their stalls, pens, coops, nests and cages.

Noah, his wife, his sons and their wives, grew weary of the crowded ark, with the not-so-pleasant animal smells. They longed to be back on land, in their homes, but the land and homes and everyone and everything else lay beneath all the water. That made Noah and his family so very sad, that creation had been destroyed.

When it finally stopped raining, Noah and his family and all the creatures had to remain in the ark for several more months, because the water stayed so high.

But God blew a wind across the dark water and the world began to dry out.

Finally, the mountain peaks peeked above the water. *Bump!* The ark came to rest on a mountaintop.

Noah released a raven and the grateful bird soared into the sky. The raven flew back and forth, back and forth, trying to find a place to land, but water still covered everything.

Next, Noah took a soft dove in his hands, and lifted it to the sky. The dove fluttered and flapped its wings and sailed off, but there was still no place to land, so it returned. Noah held out his hand to the tired dove.

A week later, Noah and the dove tried again. The dove came back with a gift in its beak: a branch from an olive tree.

"A good sign!" said Noah.

Another week later, the dove sailed off, but did not return.

"At last!" Noah shouted happily.

The ark filled with noise! Noah and his wife, their sons and wives, the birds and animals clapped and shouted and fluttered and leapt for joy.

"Time to get off the ark," God said to Noah.

"Thank you!" Noah said.

"Release the animals and birds!" God said. "Fill the world with life!"

The animals came rumbling, jumbling, tumbling off the ark and spilled out onto the land. The birds came quacking, hooting, cock-a-doodle-dooing and soared off into the cloudless sky.

Noah and his family took a deep breath of fresh, clean air and praised God.

"That will never happen again," God promised. "No matter what people do, I will not give up on them. I promise."

God's fingers spread across the sky, and an arc of colours sprang forth.

The rainbow!

"When I gaze on the earth and see the rainbow, I will remember my promise to you," God said.

When we see the rainbow, nestled in the clouds, we remember, too.

We remember that God will never give up on us.

A Son Named Laughter

As Noah had found out, when God tells you to do something, it's a good idea to listen.

Abraham was a descendant of Noah. He listened when God told him, "Leave this place that has been your home for many years. I will take you to the new land where you are to live. I will bless you. Everyone will know who you are! You will have so many children, grandchildren and great grandchildren that everyone on earth will be blessed, because of you. You will bring good into many lives. I promise."

Abraham did not know how all this would happen, but he trusted God. When God makes a promise, he keeps it, even though it might take a long time for the promise to come true.

Abraham and his wife, Sarah, were old when God spoke to them, but they did what he said. They packed up their sheep, goats, camels, cattle, donkeys, plates and cups, blankets, and tents, and began the journey to their new home. Every time they stopped along the way, Abraham worshipped God.

Finally, they arrived at the land God had promised, a land known as Canaan.

"Take a look around – look north, and south, and east, and west," God said happily. "All this land will be yours, as far as the eye can see."

Green fields like carpets rolled across the land, speckled with strong trees. Sparkling rivers watered the trees and grass, and the animals drank their cool, clear water. The land God gave Abraham could take care of his family forever.

"Can you count the specks of dust?" God then said. "Go ahead and try! It is impossible! Someday, there will be as many people in your family as there are specks of dust on the ground."

Abraham and Sarah wondered how this could be, since they had no children. But they trusted God.

They settled near a grove of oak trees. The thick, strong branches of the trees provided shade in the days when the sun shone brightly. Chattering birds nested among the leaves. Life was good.

One evening, Abraham and Sarah stretched out in their tents. They were happy, but sad, too. They wanted a baby, but were much too old to have children.

"Don't be sad," God said kindly. "I will always watch over you, and take care of you. Remember my promise. You will have as many descendants as there are stars in the sky."

So Abraham and Sarah continued to trust God and to believe God's promise, even though many people would have given up.

The sun rose and set many times, and in the blink of an eye, Abraham was nearly a hundred years old, and Sarah nearly ninety.

God reminded Abraham of his promise. "You will be the father of many, and Sarah will be the mother! Even kings will be born from your children!"

Abraham bowed to the ground and hid his face. "An old man and woman having children? That can't happen." Abraham laughed quietly, because he did not wish to be rude to God. God had kept the rest of his promise, about the land, after all.

God heard Abraham laugh. "Next year," God said, "Sarah will have a son. I will even tell you what to name him: Isaac. Do you know what that means? It means, 'laughter'." Then God went away from Abraham, and said nothing more.

Some weeks later, on a hot summer day, Sarah rested inside the tents, and Abraham sat outside in the shade, cooling off. Suddenly, three men stood nearby. He had not seen or heard them coming up the road.

Abraham sprang to his feet. He was a kind and polite man, so he ran to greet the strangers and welcome them.

"Come this way," he said, stretching out his arm towards the oaks. "Rest in the shade of my magnificent trees. I'll bring you water to wash your feet. We can have a meal together before you go on your way."

Abraham ducked under the tent flap and called to Sarah. "Visitors!" he said. "Quick, bake some bread, please!"

Sarah rubbed her sleepy eyes. "Of course," she said, for she too was kind and polite, like her husband.

Abraham ran to his servants. "Cook the best meat," he said, and they did.

He brought the meat and bread, some yoghurt and milk, and served the strange men a delicious picnic.

As they ate, one of the men said, "Where is your wife, Sarah?" He knew Sarah's name, even though they had never met.

"Inside the tent," Abraham said, "resting. She is ninety years old, after all."

The man leaned forward, and smiled. "I have wonderful news for you, Abraham. Next year, you and Sarah will have a baby boy. Your very own son."

In the tent, Sarah's ears perked up. She wrapped her wrinkled arms around her tired, old body. She felt a bubble of laughter rise up in her, and tried to hold it in, but couldn't.

"Hee, hee," the giggle escaped. She covered her mouth with her hand, and scrunched down in her robes, trying not to make a sound.

"Me, have a baby?" she said to herself. "Not only am I too old, what about Abraham? He's even older than I am! Why, that is the funniest thing I have ever heard!"

But one of the men was really God in disguise. "I heard that," he said to Abraham.

"What?" said Abraham. "What did you hear?"

"Sarah laughed. Why did she laugh? Is anything too difficult for God? Mark my words – this time next year, you will have a son."

Sarah was not laughing now. The bubble of laughter had turned into a shiver of fear. "Not me!" she hollered. "I didn't laugh!"

"Yes you did," God said. And the three men went on their way.

A year later, Abraham and Sarah laughed with joy. Their laughter rolled across the fields, green like carpets, and shook the leaves in the mighty oaks, and even reached the stars, all the many, shimmering stars. For in her arms, wrapped in a soft blanket, Sarah held their baby son.

"He is more beautiful than anything I have ever seen!" Abraham said.

Just as God had told them, they named the baby, 'Isaac'.

"How could we name him anything else?" Sarah said. "God has brought laughter into our lives. Some people will laugh at the thought of two old people having a baby, but I don't care! They will also laugh with us, because we are so happy."

So God kept the promise he had made to Abraham and Sarah.

Because God always keeps a promise.

Joseph and his Amazing Coat

Jacob, the son of Isaac, had twelve sons and one daughter. Of all his many children, Joseph was his favourite, because Jacob was very old when Joseph was born.

One day Jacob gave Joseph a special coat, more beautiful than any coat anyone had ever seen, far more handsome than anything Jacob had ever given his other sons. The coat shimmered with the colours of God's creation: vermilion, ochre, maize, emerald, periwinkle, heliotrope, magenta, sepia, ebony and cream.

"Look at me!" Joseph said to his brothers. How could they help but look at him? Everybody noticed Joseph's coat, especially his jealous brothers.

One night, Joseph had a strange dream. He could not wait to tell his brothers about it.

"Listen to my dream," he said. "We were working out in the field, gathering up bundles of wheat. My bundle was better than yours! It stood up and all of your bundles gathered in a circle around it, and bowed down."

The brothers said to Joseph, "You think you're so much better than us that you are going to rule over us like a king?"

"That dreamer!" they grumbled to each other. "Who does he think he is?"

Joseph did not seem to realise how much his brothers hated him. When he had another strange dream, he said to them, "Wait until you hear this one! In my dream last night, even the sun, moon and stars bowed to me. Eleven stars – just like my number of brothers!"

Joseph liked the dream so much he told his father, Jacob, about it, too.

"What?" said his father. "Do you expect your whole family to bow down to you, like servants?"

"That dreamer!" the brothers complained. They hated Joseph even more.

But Jacob scratched his head. "What can these dreams possibly mean?" he puzzled.

One day, the older brothers took the flocks of sheep to the fields. "Go see how your brothers are doing," Jacob told Joseph, "then come back and tell me."

Joseph put on his coat and set out to look for his brothers.

The colours on the coat shimmered in the sunlight. His brothers could see Joseph coming from far away, long before he could see them.

"That dreamer! Here he comes, to spy on us!" They boiled over with anger and jealousy.

"Let's kill him," they said. "We'll throw him into an empty well and then tell our father that a wild animal killed him. We will be rid of him once and for all!"

The oldest brother, Reuben, did not approve of the plan. "We don't need to kill him. Let's just throw him into the well and let him die there." Reuben didn't tell them that he secretly planned to come and rescue Joseph from the well once they left for home.

"Hello!" Joseph called to his brothers, waving as he came closer. He had no idea what they planned to do.

The angry, jealous brothers grabbed Joseph. They tore off his precious, colourful coat and pushed him into the well. Before Reuben could come and rescue him, a group of travelling traders passed by, and the brothers took Joseph out of the well and sold him to them as a slave.

That dreamer! He was in trouble now.

The brothers smeared Joseph's tattered coat with animal blood and took it back to their father. "Look what we found!" they said. "Doesn't this belong to Joseph?"

"Oh, no!" Jacob cried. "A wild animal must have killed him." Jacob sobbed and cried for his beloved son, and could not be comforted.

The traders took Joseph far away from his home, all the way to Egypt. They sold him to a very powerful man named Potiphar, the captain of the palace guard.

Potiphar liked Joseph. He trusted him, because he worked hard, and treated people kindly. God blessed Joseph, and so everything Joseph did, he did well. Soon, Joseph was in charge of many jobs, and Potiphar did not treat him as a slave.

Potiphar's wife, however, wanted Joseph all to herself, but Joseph refused. She was so angry that she told Potiphar, "Joseph tried to hurt me!" Potiphar believed his wife, and had Joseph thrown into jail.

Poor Joseph! But God continued to watch over him. Before long, Joseph was put in charge of the other prisoners.

Some of these prisoners had bad dreams. They woke up anxious and afraid. They told Joseph their dreams, and Joseph told them what the dreams meant. That dreamer! Now he was helping others with their dreams.

The King – the Pharaoh – began to have troubling dreams too. He could not figure out what they meant, so he called all his advisers to help. Nobody could help the Pharoah.

One of the men who had been in jail with Joseph told the Pharaoh that he knew a man who could interpret dreams. The Pharaoh had Joseph brought to him.

"I hear that you understand dreams, and can tell me their meaning," he said.

"It is not up to me," Joseph replied, "but God will tell you the meaning of the dreams through me, and perhaps that will help you feel better."

The Pharaoh told Joseph his dreams. "In the first, I stood by the Nile River, and seven plump cows came up from the water to graze in the marshes. Then, seven cows, all skin and bone, came up from the river and ate the plump cows. Yet they remained as skinny as ever, the ugliest cows I've ever seen."

"Hmmmmm. . . " murmured the dreamer.

"In the next dream, I had a stalk with seven healthy, full ears of grain growing on it. Then seven withered ears grew alongside the healthy ones and ate them up! Tell me, what do these dreams mean?"

"God is sending you an important message," Joseph answered. "For the next seven years, the land will be healthy and food will multiply. Everyone will have their fill. But for seven years after that, the land will dry up and the grain will shrivel and people will starve – unless you do something. Listen carefully to what God is saying. You need someone who can figure out a plan to keep the people of Egypt from starving. Do you know such a person?"

The Pharaoh scratched his bearded chin. "Yes, I do," he said, and looked straight at Joseph. "You." The Pharaoh made Joseph second in command in all of Egypt. Only the Pharaoh had more power.

Everything came to pass as Joseph had said it would. For seven years, the people of Egypt gathered up the grain, as plentiful as the sands on the beach, and stored it away. When the famine came, they had more than enough, so much, in fact, that people from other lands came to Egypt for help.

That is how Joseph saw his brothers again. For back home in the land of Canaan, they began to starve.

"Go to Egypt," Jacob told them. "There is food there, and we will die without it."

Joseph's brothers travelled to Egypt to beg for food. They had no clue that the man in charge of distributing the food was their very own brother, Joseph. They did not recognise him when they saw him, for many years had passed since they had thrown Joseph into the well and sold him into slavery.

Joseph recognised his brothers, and his heart thumped. He pretended not to know them, because he did not know what they might do.

The dreamer remembered the dream he'd had long ago, the eleven bundles of grain bowing down before him in the field. Here were his eleven brothers, doing just that. Joseph knew that this had been God's plan all along.

When his brothers came to Egypt a second time, they brought their youngest brother, Benjamin, at Joseph's request. Joseph and Benjamin had the same mother, and Benjamin had not been part of the plan to throw Joseph into the well all those many years before.

When Joseph saw his beloved younger brother for the first time in so many years, he had to leave the room, so he could weep without anyone seeing him. When he returned, he said to all of them, "Join me for a feast," and they did. The next day, the brothers left for home, their bellies full and their bags packed with food.

Joseph did not quite trust his brothers, after what they had done to him, so he planned a trick to see if they remained selfish and cruel. He had a silver cup hidden in Benjamin's sack of food, and after the brothers began their journey, Joseph sent one of his men after them.

"Someone has stolen a silver cup!" the man said. "That man will become a slave, while the rest of you go free. Now open your sacks so we can see who it is."

When Benjamin opened his sack, the silver cup rolled out.

The man took the brothers back to Joseph, and they bowed down in front of him. "We cannot leave our brother Benjamin here in Egypt," they said. "Our brother, Joseph, is already dead, and if anything happens to Benjamin, our dear father will die of grief."

One brother spoke up. "I will remain here in his place," he said.

Joseph saw that his brothers were now good and honest men. And Joseph, the dreamer, broke down and cried in front of them all.

"Look at me!" he sobbed and wept. "I am your brother, Joseph, the one you sold into slavery so long ago. The evil you tried to do to me, God meant for good, for see, I am here now to save you from starving."

Joseph! Could it be? The brothers hardly believed their eyes and ears.

"Now go back home," Joseph said, "and bring our father here, and your wives and sons and daughters, so we can all be together again." The brothers hugged and kissed one another with joy. They all bowed down before Joseph.

They travelled back to Canaan and returned to Egypt with Jacob and all the family, right down to the youngest child. Having the family all together again was like a wonderful dream come true.

And as time passed, Jacob's family multiplied like the stars in the sky, just as God had promised Abraham long, long ago.

The Baby in the Basket

God's people, the Hebrews, lived in Egypt for many years after Joseph's entire family settled in the land. Soon, there were so many of them that the new Pharaoh became nervous. He feared that the Hebrews would be stronger than his own armies, and turn against him.

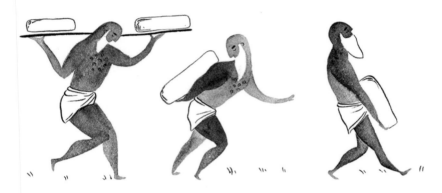

"We must do something about these people," he said to his fellow Egyptians. They decided to turn the Hebrews into slaves and make them do all the hardest work.

Still, the Hebrews multiplied and became stronger. So the Pharaoh gave an order. "Whenever a Hebrew woman gives birth to a son, the baby should be killed at once!"

But nobody was willing to do such a terrible thing. The Pharaoh, angered by their refusal, spoke to all the Egyptians. "If any boys are born to the Hebrews, throw them into the Nile River at once!"

A Hebrew woman named Jochebed gave birth to a beautiful, healthy baby boy. She could not bear to think of anyone throwing him into the river, so she hid him as long as she could. Then she made a basket from the reeds in the nearby marsh, coated it with resin to make it waterproof, and placed her son in the basket. She hid the baby in the basket by the edge of the Nile River, hoping she could keep him safe and out of sight.

The baby's older sister, Miriam, loved her little brother. She hid nearby and watched to see what would happen to him.

A rustling sound startled her. Somebody was approaching! Miriam crouched down further in the reeds.

She could not believe her eyes. Stepping into the water to bathe was none other than the Pharaoh's grown daughter, the Princess.

"That basket over there? Do you see it?" the Princess asked her handmaidens who had come to help her bathe. "Bring it to me!"

Miriam held her breath, and waited quietly to see what would happen.

The Princess opened the basket, and a loud wail came from inside. "A baby!" she cried. "A beautiful baby boy!"

The Princess's heart melted at the sight. "He must belong to one of the Hebrew women," she said. And rather than throw him into the river as her father had ordered, she told everyone, "I will raise him as my own son."

Brave Miriam saw her chance. She stood up where she was hiding. "Shall I go and find a Hebrew woman to nurse the baby until he has grown bigger?" she suggested.

"Yes," agreed the Princess. So Miriam ran home to her mother, the baby's own mother, and brought her to the Princess.

"Take this baby and nurse him for me," said the Princess. "When he is older I shall send for him."

So the baby lived with his family for several years, then went to live with the Princess at the palace. She was good to him and loved him as if he were her own child.

"I shall call you Moses," she said, which means, "to pull out of the water."

Moses grew up at the palace, and was well cared for, but his Hebrew family never forgot him, and he never forgot them.

As he grew up, he witnessed his fellow Hebrews being ill-treated. One day, Moses saw an Egyptian cruelly beating one of the Hebrews, and in his anger, he killed the Egyptian. He tried to hide what he had done, but eventually, the Pharaoh found out. "Kill Moses!" he shouted in anger.

Moses ran far away, to a land called Midian. There he married a woman called Zipporah, and they had a son. Moses spent his time taking care of the many sheep that belonged to his wife's father, Jethro.

Years passed. Back in Egypt, a new Pharaoh became King, and was just as cruel as the one before him. The Hebrew people sighed and groaned. "Help us!" they cried to God, "Please help us!"

Just as Moses did not forget his Hebrew family when he lived in the Pharaoh's palace, God did not forget his people. He heard their cries for help, and remembered the promise he had made with Abraham, Isaac and Jacob, to watch over them and care for them. God burned with anger at the way the Hebrews were being treated by the Egyptians.

One day while out caring for the sheep, Moses came to the foot of a mountain known as the Mountain of God.

Something strange caught his eye. It was a bush – on fire! Moses ran to investigate, but when he looked more closely at the bush, he saw something strange. The flames were blazing, but he realised the

bush did not burn up.

Then Moses heard a voice coming from the bush.

"Moses! Moses!" the voice called.

"Here I am!" Moses replied, not knowing who it was that called to him.

"Take off your shoes," said the voice. "This ground is holy ground."

Moses took off his shoes.

"I am the God of Abraham, the God of Isaac and the God of Jacob," said the voice.

For the voice did not belong to just anybody. It belonged to God! Moses trembled with fear.

"I have heard the voices of my people in Egypt, crying for help, and I have come to their aid. I need you to take them from Egypt back home to the land I promised to their ancestors."

"Who, me?" said Moses, and then, "Why me? What if the people do not believe me? What if they ask me your name? What should I tell them?"

"I AM WHO I AM," God said. "I WILL BE WHAT I WILL BE. Tell them that I AM has sent you to take them home."

Moses had never heard such a name. He did not think that he could do what God asked. "Isn't there someone else you can send who will know what to do?"

God's voice thundered with anger, because Moses did not believe him. "Your brother, Aaron, is coming to visit you soon. I will tell you what to say, and you will tell Aaron, and he will tell the people. We will do this together."

Moses could not argue with that.

God intended to lead his people back to their homeland. And the baby in the basket, the man who heard God in the burning bush, was just the man for the job.

The Ten Plagues Of Egypt

After Moses talked to God in the burning bush, he returned to Egypt with his wife and sons and his brother, Aaron. They gathered all the leaders of the Hebrews. "God has heard your cries," Aaron told them. "He has commanded Moses to lead you home, away from this place."

"Praise God!" the people responded.

Moses and Aaron went to the Pharaoh. "The Lord, the God of Israel has a message for you, and the message is this: Let my people go."

"You can't be serious," Pharaoh answered. "I do not know this God of whom you speak. Why should I let the people go? Who would do their work? My answer is no! I will not let the people go."

And because the Pharaoh's heart was stubborn and hard, he made the work of the Hebrews even more difficult. The people blamed Moses. "Why should we listen to you? Our lives are even worse than before!"

"What do I do now?" Moses asked God.

"I will show the Pharaoh that I am the Lord, the God of the Hebrews," said God.

So God sent ten plagues to try and convince the Pharaoh to let the Hebrews leave Egypt.

First, the Nile River turned to blood. The fish died and the Egyptians could no longer drink. But the Pharaoh would not change his mind.

So then God sent frogs. Frogs, frogs and more frogs. They hopped into beds so nobody could sleep and they hopped into ovens so the people could not bake their bread. The frogs covered everything.

"I hate frogs!" yelled the Pharaoh. "You can leave now, Moses, and take the people – and the frogs – with you."

But once the frogs were gone, the Pharaoh changed his mind and would not let the people go.

"Strike your staff on the ground," God said to Moses, and when Moses did, the dust turned into gnats.

Millions of nasty gnats swarmed the land and drove the people crazy. The gnats were worse than the frogs!

The Pharaoh said, "No! You may not leave."

Flies replaced the gnats. They buzzed in people's ears and eyes and noses. and made everyone miserable. Then all the working animals of the Egyptians died of disease.

Still the Pharaoh said, "No! You're not going anywhere! Get back to work!"

Next, boils broke out on everyone's skin. The Pharaoh's heart got harder and harder and he would not let the people go.

Hailstones thundered from the sky and pounded the earth. Swarms of locusts ate the fruit and leaves off of all the trees. Then a terrible darkness covered the land like a thick blanket and nobody could see anything. But did the Pharaoh change his mind? No!

So God said, "I will bring one last plague on Egypt. It will be so terrible that Pharaoh will let you go. At midnight tonight, every firstborn son in Egypt will die, from the firstborn son of the Pharaoh to that of the poorest female slave."

And it happened just as God said.

"GET OUT!" the Pharaoh finally said to Moses, full of grief at the death of his firstborn son. "Get out and never come back!"

"Time to go home," God told his people. As they left, he led them with a large cloud during the day and at night, a brilliant flame of fire.

But no sooner had Moses and the Hebrews started their journey than the Pharaoh changed his mind again. "Chase them down!" he said, and the entire army loaded up in

their chariots and raced after Moses and the people.

"Save us!" the people cried to God when they saw all those Egyptians rushing towards them. They had camped near the seashore and had nowhere to go to escape the Egyptians.

"Never fear," said Moses, and he raised his hand. A mighty wind sent by God blew a pathway through the water.

"Hurry!" Moses ordered.

The Hebrews rushed along the path, between towering walls of water. The Egyptians in their speedy chariots came closer and closer. As soon as the Hebrews made it safely to the other side, Moses raised his hand again, and the walls of water crashed down upon the Egyptians and swept them out to sea.

The Hebrews fell to their knees in wonder, and worshipped God. Miriam, the sister that had watched the Princess rescue her baby brother, Moses, from the Nile River so many years before, sang and danced with joy at the goodness of God.

If only the rest of the journey had been easy! But that was not to be.

Month after month, year after year, the people trudged along.

They had no homes. They got discouraged, and kept trying to do

things their own way, instead of God's. "We don't like this!" The people complained. "We want to go back to Egypt!"

Time and time again, God had to remind them that he was God, not them. God made the sky rain with small bits of bread to feed them when they were hungry. "You are my children," God told them through Aaron and Moses. "I love you and will always take care of you."

When they continued to turn away from God, he called Moses to the top of a great mountain. Lightning flashed and thunder crashed and both Moses and the mountain trembled. "I have some rules for you to give to my people," God said. The most important rules are these: Love me with your whole being. Remember the Sabbath day – the day when I rested after creating the whole world. Don't kill or steal or lie or wish you had something that belongs to someone else."

God gave them these commandments so they could learn to live peacefully with one another and to follow him.

The trip to the Promised Land of Canaan took forty long years, but the people finally arrived home. Moses died right before they got there, but he had done his job, just as God had asked him to do.

David And Goliath

The Hebrew people, also known as the people of Israel, had returned to the land that God had promised to them long before. They had a king, named Saul. But God wasn't happy with Saul. God wanted a person who had a heart like him – a heart filled with love – to be the king of his people.

God sent Samuel to a little town called Bethlehem. Samuel was the one who would select a new king. "Go and see a man named Jesse," God told him. "I have chosen one of Jesse's sons to be the king."

Samuel travelled across the hills and valleys to Bethlehem. When he arrived at Jesse's house, he said, "Come with me, and bring your sons. We will eat, and then worship God together."

When Jesse's eldest son appeared, Samuel thought, "He is tall and strong and handsome! He must be the one whom God has chosen to be king."

But God said to him, "Don't pay attention to how someone looks on the outside. I see what a person is like on the inside. I choose a man who has a loving heart, like mine."

Jesse's second son came out to meet Samuel. "Nope," Samuel said.

The third son took his turn. "Next!" Samuel said.

Seven sons passed by Samuel, and seven times Samuel said, "Nope," or "Next!" or "Not this one."

Then Samuel asked Jesse, "Is that all of your sons?"

Jesse paused. "There is one more, the youngest, David," he answered. "He is out in the field, taking care of the sheep."

"What are you waiting for?" said Samuel. "Bring him here!"

As soon as he saw David, Samuel announced, "That's the one!"

David had beautiful eyes, and was handsome like his brothers, but he had a loving heart like God, and God loved him. In fact, the name, 'David', means 'beloved'.

But David did not become king right away. Saul remained in charge, but he was deeply troubled. An army of warriors known as the Philistines fought against the

people of Israel, killing them left and right. None of the king's men could stop them. Their mightiest warrior, Goliath, towered above everyone else, for he was as tall and strong as a mighty tree. Not five feet tall. Not six feet tall. Not even eight feet tall, but ten feet tall!

"Send me your strongest man to fight!" hollered Goliath. "If he wins, we will be your slaves, but if I win, you will belong to us!"

The people of Israel trembled with fear.

For forty days, Goliath bellowed at the people. "Come out and fight!" But nobody wanted to fight Goliath, including Jesse's sons. "Nope," they said. "Not us!"

David was too young to fight with the army. Instead, he took care of his father's sheep. Jesse worried about his other sons, so he told David, "Go, and take food and supplies to your brothers who are fighting the Philistines. Send word to let me know if they are okay."

Once at the army camp, David heard a roar that sounded like thunder. Goliath! The hills shook at the sound of his voice, and everyone scattered and ran away.

Everyone, that is, except David.

"I will fight this man!" David said.

"You?" said his brothers.

"You?" said the king.

"Me." David said. "I know how to take care of the sheep. When lions or bears try to kill one of my lambs, I stop them. The God who saves me from the paw of the lion and the paw of the bear will protect me against Goliath!"

King Saul gave David his finest armour, but David was not used to wearing the heavy items and took them off. "I cannot fight with these," he said.

Instead, David took his shepherd's staff. He knelt in a green meadow by a stream of peaceful water. One by one, he plucked five round, smooth stones from the stream. *Thunk!* He dropped the stones in a leather pouch and slung it over his shoulder. In his hand, he held his trusty catapult.

"I'm ready," said David.

"He is doomed!" groaned the people. "That means we are doomed, too!"

David, the shepherd boy, the future king, the one who had a heart like God, did not fear the mighty Goliath. He marched straight towards him.

Goliath did not fear David, either, although he should have. Instead, he was enraged when he saw the young boy standing before him without any armour and without any weapons.

"Who do you think you are?" Goliath shouted. "Do you think I am a dog? Have you come to chase me away with sticks?" Goliath cursed God, which made David angry.

David did not shake with fear. He did not run away. "I come to you in the name of the Lord God!" David yelled at Goliath, which made Goliath even angrier.

The ground shook as Goliath stomped towards the young shepherd boy. David grabbed a stone from his pouch, placed it in his catapult, and whirled it around his head.

Whoosh! The stone flew through the air.

Thwack! It smacked Goliath in the forehead.

Crash! Goliath fell to the ground, dead.

When the rest of the Philistines saw their mighty hero lying on the ground, they turned and ran away as fast as their frightened legs could carry them.

So the young shepherd boy, the boy with a loving heart like God, saved the people.

David became a great king, and under his rule, Israel became a mighty nation. The people loved him, and so did God. After all, that is what the name, 'David' means. Beloved.

Jonah And The Big Fish

This story started because of a city called Nineveh. Nineveh was a great city, but the people weren't very nice. In fact, they were downright wicked. They paid no attention to God – at all.

"I want you to go to Nineveh," the Lord God said to a man called Jonah. "Tell them that they have made me angry, and if they don't change their ways, they will be destroyed."

Did Jonah do what God asked him to do?

No! He hopped on the nearest boat, but not to Nineveh. Jonah didn't like the Ninevites, and thought they deserved what was coming to them. He wanted to get as far from that place as he could, so he headed in the opposite direction. Did he think he could hide from God? Adam and Eve had tried that, and that didn't work out too well. Nobody can hide from God.

Still, Jonah thought he'd try. "I'll take this boat to Tarshish. Nobody will ever know."

But God knew. God hurled a powerful wind across the sea, and the waves crashed, splashed, bashed and nearly smashed that boat to smithereens, which is to say, lots of bits and pieces.

The sailors on the boat wept and wailed and prayed to their gods, "Save us!" They threw boxes, bins and anything they could get their hands on right over the side of the boat.

Their gods did not answer. The crashing, splashing, bashing and nearly smashing kept on until they feared that they all would die.

And Jonah? He slept through it all! The captain found him tucked into his bed deep down in the boat, snoring.

"Get up!" the captain hollered. "Pray to your God to save us. Maybe he will listen. Our gods aren't doing a thing to help."

Jonah rubbed the sleep from his eyes. "Uh, oh," he said. "This is my fault. I worship the God who made the heavens, the land and the sea. I am running away from God, and trying to hide from him." Jonah sighed. "There is only one way to stop the storm. You must throw me overboard."

The sailors did not want to do this to Jonah. They tried rowing to land, they tried praying to Jonah's God. The storm continued to rage. Finally, they saw they had no choice but to do what Jonah said.

They pitched Jonah right over the side of the boat. Immediately all the crashing, splashing, bashing, and nearly smashing stopped. Just like that.

"Wow!" the sailors said. "From now on, we are going to worship Jonah's God!"

But what happened to Jonah?

He sank down, down, down into the deep blue sea.

Just when he could no longer hold his breath, along came a very large fish and GULP! That fish swallowed Jonah right up! That's how big a fish it was.

"Whew," thought Jonah. Then, "phew!" It does not smell very good inside the belly of a smelly fish.

For three days and three nights, Jonah sloshed around inside that fish.

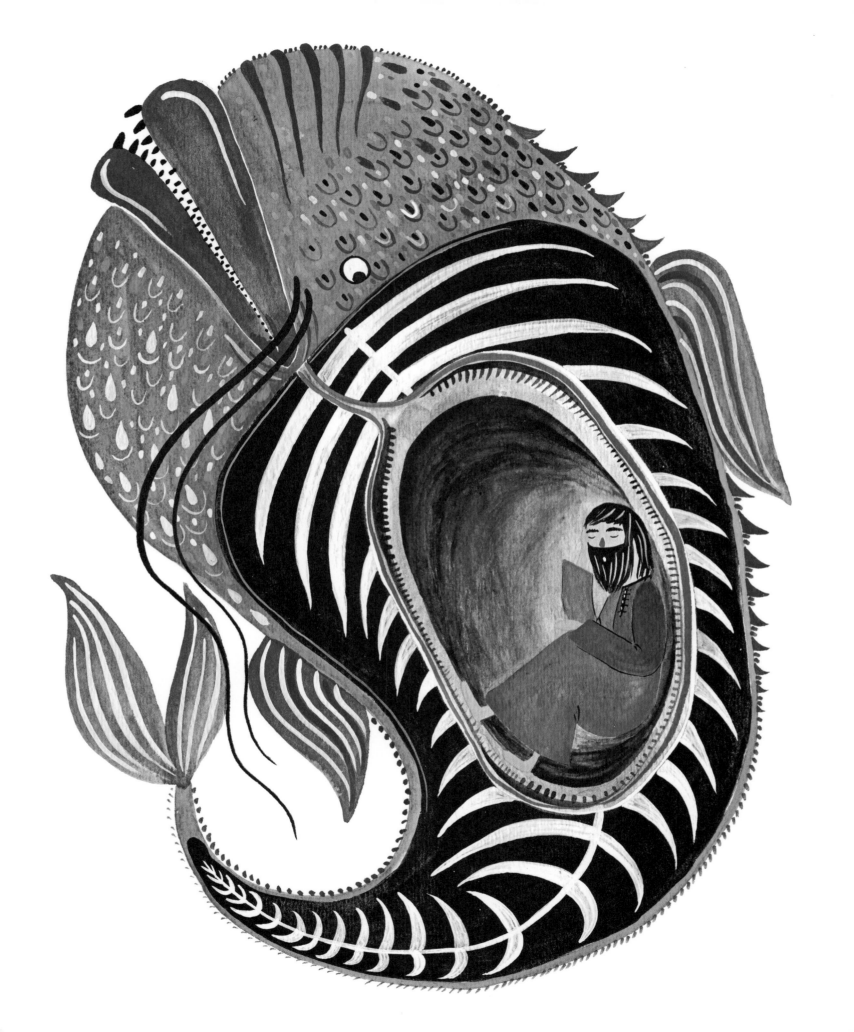

Pitch dark, he could see nothing. He had plenty of time to think about what he had done.

"Please, God," he said. "Get me out of here. I won't try and hide from you any more."

God told the fish to spit out Jonah, and the fish did. Up, up, up came Jonah, right onto dry land.

"Are you ready to go to Nineveh now, and give them my message?" God asked.

"Yes!" Jonah said, so relieved to be out of that smelly belly. "I will do whatever you say. I promise."

This time, Jonah was true to his word. He'd learned his lesson.

Jonah walked the streets of Nineveh, shouting to the people, "Mend your ways! Turn back to God, or in forty days, you will all be destroyed!" It took Jonah three days to walk the city of Nineveh, the same amount of time he'd been inside that fish.

Word gets around, and the king of Nineveh heard about Jonah and the big fish. "Let all the people of Nineveh turn from their evil ways, and follow God!" the king proclaimed. "Perhaps God will save us."

And sure enough, God did.

Jonah should have been happy that God decided to save the people of Nineveh. But was he? No!

He got angry.

"Humph," he grumbled. "They don't deserve to be saved by God."

Then Jonah said to God, "I knew this would happen! I knew you would be forgiving. That's why I didn't want to go to Nineveh. Just go ahead and kill me."

"What is wrong with you, Jonah?" God asked. "You should be happy about this."

Jonah stomped off, marching right out of Nineveh. He built himself a little shelter on a hill, and plopped down where he could look at the city and see what God would do next.

God caused a vine to grow up over Jonah to give him shade from the hot, dry sun. Jonah was grateful.

But then God sent a worm to eat the vine, so Jonah no longer had shade. The sun beat down on him until he fainted. When he woke, he shouted, "Let me die!"

"Are you so angry about losing a vine?" God asked him.

"Yes!" Jonah shouted. "I am angry about that vine, angry enough that I want to die."

"You didn't make that vine," God said to him, "or plant or water it, and yet you are angry enough that it's gone to want to die. How do you think I feel about Nineveh? Aren't the people of that great city worth more than a vine? But you didn't feel sad to think they might all be lost. And you didn't want me to save them."

And Jonah had no answer for that.

The New Testament

Jesus is Born

In the village of Nazareth lived a girl named Mary. She had a pure and strong spirit, and held a special place in God's heart.

Mary lived at home, awaiting the day when she would marry Joseph, a good and kind man who worked as a carpenter. Suddenly, rainbows of light shimmered in Mary's room, and – out of nowhere – an angel appeared!

"Greetings!" said the angel, whose name was Gabriel. "The Lord is with you! Of all the women in the world, you are most blessed."

Gabriel's sudden appearance startled Mary, and the words left her troubled. "What can this mean?" she wondered.

"Do not be afraid, Mary," the angel said gently. "You have a special place in God's heart, and so you have been chosen to give birth to God's very own Son. You will name him 'Jesus', which means, 'God saves us'. He will rule over the entire earth, and his kingdom will never end!"

Mary was puzzled. "I'm not sure how I can have a baby," she said to Gabriel. "Joseph and I are engaged, but we are not yet married."

"Joseph will not be the father of your child. God will be," said Gabriel. "The Holy Spirit will surround you like a shining cloud, and the baby will grow inside you, like all babies do. In fact, your relative, Elizabeth, is also having a baby, even though she is very old. Nothing is impossible with God."

Mary believed the angel, and rejoiced. "I am God's servant, and will do whatever he asks of me," she said. Gabriel vanished as quickly as he had appeared.

"I must go and see Elizabeth," Mary thought. "She will understand."

Mary hurried down dusty roads and scurried up hills to where Elizabeth and her husband, Zechariah lived. Elizabeth opened the door, surprised to see Mary standing there.

"Elizabeth!" Mary said, and threw her arms around her. At the sound of Mary's voice, the baby inside Elizabeth jumped for joy.

"Oh!" Elizabeth said. "My baby knows who you are – the mother of God's Son. You are blessed because you believed God's promise."

Mary stayed with Elizabeth for three months, to help care for her. Shortly after Mary returned home, Elizabeth gave birth to her son, John, who later became known as John the Baptist.

When Joseph heard that Mary was going to have a baby before they were married, he was shocked and hurt. What was he going to do now?

So God sent an angel to him in a dream. "Do not be afraid, Joseph," the angel told him. "Go ahead and get married, as you planned. Mary's baby is a holy child, God's Son. All will be well."

When the morning light dawned, Joseph awoke. He no longer felt afraid, for he trusted in God.

Everything came to pass as the angel Gabriel said it would. The time flew by quickly and Mary's baby grew until it was time for him to be born.

At that time, the Roman emperor, Caesar Augustus, ruled over many nations, including Israel. He decided to count all the people who lived in the land. Everyone had to go back to the place where their relatives had come from. Joseph and Mary travelled the long journey to Bethlehem, where Joseph's great-great grandfather, King David had lived. David was the beloved king who had saved his people from the mighty Goliath.

But Joseph and Mary weren't the only ones travelling to Bethlehem. When they arrived, they found that every house was filled to overflowing.

"Joseph!" groaned Mary, clutching her tummy. "This baby is coming. Now!"

Poor Joseph felt desperate! He went from door to door. "Please," he said. "My wife is about to have a baby. We need a place to stay."

"Sorry, we have no room," everyone told him. Even the inn in town had no place to put them.

Joseph knew he had to find a safe place for Mary and the baby. But where?

Then, in the deepening darkness, Joseph heard murmurings from close by. *Mooooo! Baaaaa!*

Joseph recognised the familiar sounds of cows and sheep settling into their shelter for the night. "Ah ha!" he thought. "Here is a safe place for Mary, among the animals."

There was no time to waste. Joseph hurried Mary to the stable and made her a bed in the straw.

Starlight shone through the open windows. Cows blinked their big, brown eyes, and their soft breath warmed the cool air. Hens clucked, and tucked their baby chicks beneath their feathered bellies. Woolly sheep bumbled and stumbled, trying to get a look at the visitors. Camels crunched and munched their evening meal of hay.

And right there among the animals, Mary gave birth to the baby Jesus.

"Oh, Joseph," she sighed, exhausted, when she saw her son for the first time. "He's beautiful!"

Joseph wiped a tear from his eye. "Yes," he smiled. "The most beautiful baby ever!"

Mary wrapped Jesus in bands of cloth, and placed him in the manger, the animal's feeding trough, as if it were a cradle.

God's joyful laugh bounced through the heavens, echoing across the clouds. Stars burst across the sky like sparkling fireworks, and all the angels spun and danced with happiness.

Not too far away, out in the fields, a group of scraggly shepherds gazed over their flocks of sheep, counting each one to be sure they were all safe for the night. "What's that sound?" one asked another. "Like a flock of birds rustling in the trees, but there are no birds out this late at night."

The rustling sound grew louder and louder until ... *Whoosh!* An angel with mighty wings landed right in the midst of the startled shepherds. The angel flashed and shone with God's glory.

"Wh-wh-what's that?" they said to each other, and fell down in fear, covering their faces with their hands.

"Do not be afraid!" the angel said. "I am here with good news. Great news. The best news in the whole world!"

The shepherds peeked through their fingers as the angel continued.

"God's Son – the saviour of the world – is born! Today! Just now! Not far from here, in Bethlehem. Go and see for yourselves! You'll know you've found him when you see a baby sleeping in a manger."

The angels of heaven could no longer silence their joy. Their jubilant song of praise shook the sky as they sang:

"Glory to God in the highest heaven,

and peace to those who have found favour with God."

The angels swirled and vanished back into heaven.

"What are we waiting for?" the shepherds asked one another. "Let's go to Bethlehem! We must see this wonder that the angels have told us about."

They stumbled to that humble shelter and found the baby Jesus, just as the angels had told them. A soft light glowed around him.

"You won't believe what just happened!" they said to the people who had gathered outside the stable when they heard that a baby had been born. "An angel told us that this is God's Son!"

Everyone who heard this marvelled at the news. "Can this be true?" they asked one another.

Mary kept all their words tucked safely in the pocket of her heart, to think about more deeply as time passed.

Off the shepherds went, back to their fields and their flocks, dancing and singing in the starlight, praising God who had decided to tell them this good news.

Far, far away, in another land east of Israel, a group of very wise men who studied the stars noticed one brighter than any star they had ever seen before. "A new king has just been born," they said. "We must go to see him."

They travelled many long miles, over dunes of windswept sand, across valleys, up mountains and down, following the star until they came to Jerusalem, the capital city of Israel. "Where is the new king?" they asked. "We saw his star rise in the east and have come to worship him. Can someone tell us where he is?"

The king, Herod, did not like this at all. He did not want there to be another king besides him! He asked all the well-educated religious leaders in Jerusalem to figure out when and where this baby had been born, so that he could kill him.

"Many long years ago, our prophet, a man who spoke for God, said that God's chosen king would be born in Bethlehem," the men told Herod.

Frightened and furious, Herod sent for the wise men who had come from eastern lands to find this baby.

"Go and find this king," Herod said, "and once you have discovered where he lives, come back and let me know so I can worship him, too."

The wise men left Jerusalem and followed the brilliant star to Bethlehem where they found Mary, Joseph and baby Jesus.

The wise men could barely hold in their joy at finding this king who had long ago been promised by God. They entered the house where Mary, Joseph and Jesus had been living since Jesus' birth, and knelt down before them.

"We have come from very far away to meet the king. We have brought gifts."

They opened their treasure bags, and showed the family the special presents: gleaming, glittering gold; valuable, sweet-smelling frankincense; and myrrh, a rare perfume. All these were gifts that one would give to a king.

That night, as the wise men slept before beginning their long journey home, they had a dream, which warned them to stay away from the wicked King Herod, who wanted to kill Jesus. So they did not go back through Jerusalem, but took a different route.

After they left, Joseph had another dream, and in that dream an angel of God warned him about Herod's plans. So Joseph took Mary and Jesus and they travelled to Egypt, far away from Herod. They stayed in Egypt until Herod died, and they could return home safely.

The Sermon on the Mount

Joseph, Mary and Jesus returned to Nazareth following their escape to Egypt. Jesus grew up with his family, much like any other child. But Mary and Joseph never forgot that he was special. When he became a grown man, it was time for Jesus to leave them and begin teaching about God's love.

His relative, John the Baptist, baptised him in the Jordan River. Then Jesus chose twelve men, called disciples, to follow him. The disciples travelled everywhere he went, and learned from him as he taught others.

Jesus taught in people's homes, in boats and in the places of worship, the synagogues. Sometimes, when the crowds were so big the people could not fit in a building, Jesus taught along the seashore, or in a field. He healed many who were sick. He listened to those who were sad, or lonely. More and more people heard the stories about Jesus, and huge crowds began to follow him wherever he went.

"Look at that crowd!" the disciples said to Jesus. "All these people want to get close to you, to learn about God's love."

"Come with me," he said to everyone. The people followed him up a mountainside, and gathered around him. The sky shone a periwinkle blue, and a soft, gentle breeze cooled their faces, which were all turned towards Jesus. The air smelled sweet with the scent of lilies and roses, and birds dressed in brilliant ruby reds and dazzling yellows twittered and chirped in the trees.

Jesus gazed around at the people. Some could not walk and had to be carried up the mountain by their friends. Others had tears in their eyes because a loved one had died. Many were poor, and had very little to call their own. All of them longed to hear his healing words, or to feel his healing touch.

"Hear this good news," Jesus said to them all. "I have gathered you here to tell you how to live a life full of God's blessings.

"Do you feel worthless?" Jesus asked the crowd. "You are not. Heaven belongs to you. God bless you!

"Are you sad? God will comfort you, always. God bless you!

"Those of you who are humble will inherit the whole earth. God bless you!

"If you are hungry and thirsty to know more about God, God's love will fill you up. God bless you!

"Be loving and kind to all, and you will also receive love and kindness. God bless you!

"If your heart is gentle and honest, you will see God. God bless you!

"Be peaceful, and try hard to bring peace into the world so you can be called God's children. God bless you!

"Don't worry if people make fun of you or treat you unkindly because you believe in God. Loving God is more important than what others think of you. God welcomes you into his kingdom. God bless you!"

The people heard, and believed what Jesus said.

A man who could not walk looked around at his friends who had carried him there, and felt blessed. He reached out and held the hand of a woman who had tears in her eyes because her husband had died, and she felt a glimmer of joy. She reached into her pocket and took out the bread she had carried with her, and gave it to the hungry child sitting nearby. The child shared with her brothers, so they would stop quarrelling.

People looked around at strangers who had come from other places, and they smiled at one another, and said, "God bless you."

"Think of yourselves as salt," Jesus said. "What does salt do?"

"Gives our food flavour!" called out one person.

"Preserves it!" said another. (This was before refrigerators, and salt helped keep food fresh.)

"You are like that," said Jesus. "Your faith in God gives life flavour, because you bring joy and kindness and peace into the world. Your faith preserves the good things that God wants for everyone. So keep learning about God and share your faith with other people. That is what it means to be the salt of the earth."

Then Jesus asked, "What about light? What does light do?"

"Helps us find our way in the dark!" the people cried out.

"Exactly!" Jesus said. "Would you hide a lamp under a basket? No! What is the good in that? You would put your lamp on a table so it will give light to everyone in the house.

"You are light," he continued. "Just like the light helps people find their way in the dark, you can help people find their way to God. Be kind to others. Do good deeds in God's name, and that shows people what God is like."

"We can do that!" the people agreed.

"Does this mean I can never get angry at anyone?" a girl asked.

"We all get angry at times," Jesus said. "But don't let your anger take over. If someone hurts your feelings, or if you do something mean to another person, try to work it out. Don't give up. Keep trying until you can forgive each other. Even people you think are your enemies."

"It's so much easier to be nice to people who are nice to me," a young boy said.

"Anyone can do that!" said Jesus. "But God wants you to love everyone, even those with whom you do not agree."

"What about my enemies?" another asked.

"Even your enemies," Jesus answered. "Be different from the rest of the world, from those who fight and call names and don't want to forgive. Don't believe the old saying, 'an eye for an eye and a tooth for a tooth'. God expects more from you. Instead, if someone hits your cheek, turn the other cheek towards them too.

"Here is a way to think about it," Jesus went on. "Treat other people the way you want them to treat you. Think about what you say and do before you say and do it. Put yourself in the other person's place."

"Can you teach us how to pray?"

"You don't need big, fancy words," Jesus said. "Think of prayer as having a conversation with someone you love, who loves you, too. God listens and wants you to share everything in your heart. He already knows what you need.

"Pray like this:

God in heaven, your name is holy.

Let your light shine in the world, like it does in heaven.

Give us just what we need for this day.

Forgive us for doing what is wrong,

And help us forgive people who have hurt us.

Keep us safe and give us strength when we are tempted to do what we are not supposed to do."

A flock of birds soared through the sky as Jesus finished the first Lord's Prayer.

"It's easy to worry about so many things in life," said Jesus. "But look at those birds! See how happy they are! They aren't worried about anything. God gives them seeds and bugs to eat every day. If God feeds the birds, don't you think that God watches over you, too?

"Now, look over there!" Jesus pointed at the fields of snow-white lilies dancing in the afternoon breeze. "Aren't they beautiful? Do you think the lilies worry about

what they're going to wear each day?"

Children giggled, and even the adults couldn't help but laugh at that thought.

"Of course not!" Jesus said. "God clothes the lilies in beauty, even more glorious than the robes and jewels of a great king! So don't worry about what you're going to wear. Worrying is useless. Follow me, and love God, and you will have everything you need."

Jesus continued to teach for the entire rest of the day, and nobody minded, because everything he said was clothed in wisdom and truth.

Four Faithful Friends

"Hurry! Hurry! He's back! Let's go see!"

Clouds of dust rose in the streets as people poured out of their homes, hurrying and scurrying towards the house where Jesus lived but rarely spent any time, with all the travelling he did. But today, he was home! People came from shops and homes and fields and even the nearby villages to see Jesus, to hear his words, to be healed.

One man, however, could not run to see Jesus. He could not even walk to him, because his legs were paralysed, and did not work. He lay on his side on a thick mat, watching all the people run past.

"I wonder what it feels like to walk!" he wondered. "I can't imagine anything more wonderful in the whole, wide world!"

He closed his eyes, and imagined running down the street, across the town, right up to the very top of a mountain.

And suddenly, *whoosh!* He felt himself being lifted from the ground. What in the world? He looked up and into the faces of his four best friends, who each held a corner of his mat.

"We're taking you to Jesus!" they said.

By the time they reached the house, the crowds had become as thick as stew. People stood toe to toe inside. They jammed inside the doorway, trying to get closer to Jesus.

"Excuse us, please!" the four friends pleaded, but nobody moved away.

That didn't stop them.

People began to climb up on top of the roof, leaning over the edges, hoping to at least hear a word or two from Jesus.

"It's no use," the paralysed man said to his friends. "There's no way we can get close."

"We are not giving up!" the four friends insisted. Carefully, they lifted the man on the mat up onto the roof.

"Jesus can't see us up here," the man said.

That didn't stop them.

Inside the house, clods of dirt thumped onto the heads of several people. *Plop!* "What's going on?" they squawked, brushing the dirt off their heads and faces. Looking up, they saw four faces peering down at them. The friends had dug a hole, right through the roof!

"Make way!" they shouted. People stood aside as a ragged mat with a man lying on it was slowly lowered by ropes into the room. *Plop!* It landed right at the feet of Jesus.

The crowd hushed. Would Jesus be angry that the men had cut a hole in his roof? Would he shush them, send them away?

Jesus smiled, and it seemed the very sun lit up the room. "Such good and faithful friends!" he said. "You did not let anything stop you from bringing your friend to me."

He shifted his gaze to the man lying on the mat. "Take heart," he said. "Your sins are forgiven. It is not your fault that your legs don't work."

And what happened next? Did the crowd jump for joy at Jesus' words?

No! In fact, the ones who didn't like Jesus mumbled and grumbled.

"Who does he think he is?" they whispered. "Only God can say such things! Jesus has no right to forgive anyone!"

Jesus knew full well what they were thinking. "Why do you think such cruel and angry thoughts?" he asked, but they would not answer him.

The people might be heartless. They might not approve of Jesus. But that didn't stop him from doing what he had been sent by God to do.

Again, Jesus looked at the man, lying on the mat before him.

"To show you that I do have the right to forgive, and to do God's work here on earth, listen to this!"

He held out his arms to the man who could not walk and said in a voice that echoed off the walls, out the door and through the roof, "Stand up! Pick up your mat and go home. Walk home."

The man sprang to his feet, which had never held him up before. He flexed one straight, strong leg, and then the other. He hopped from one foot to the other. He looked at Jesus, eye to eye, the first time he had ever been able to do that.

He stood still for a moment. A smile crept from deep within him, and his face shone. Then he couldn't help himself – he jumped for joy!

The crowds pressed around him, wanting to get a closer look. But the man wanted to go home. He rolled up his mat and tucked it under his arm. "Excuse me," he said. People stepped aside so he could pass through. The man, no longer on the mat, marched right out the door on his very own two legs.

"Amazing!" the people shouted. "We've never seen anything like this! God is great! Praise God forever!"

And the four faithful friends?

Their smiles were the biggest of all. Their friend, who had been paralysed, could walk. A miracle! They knew now – and so did the rest of the crowd – that nothing could stop Jesus from sharing God's love.

Jesus Feeds Five Thousand People

One day, Jesus received some very sad news. His relative, John the Baptist, had been killed. John was the baby that had jumped for joy in his mother's womb when Mary first learned that she was going to be the mother of Jesus. After they had grown up, John had baptised Jesus in the Jordan River.

Jesus' heart broke when he heard about John's death. He needed time alone to grieve, and to pray. He walked down to the nearby sea, got into a small boat, and began to row to the other side.

The gentle waves lapped the side of the boat. Jesus remembered the feel of the cold water swirling around him as John baptised him. He would never forget the sight of the Holy Spirit coming down from the heavens like a beautiful white dove, and the joyful sound of his Father's voice from heaven, saying, "This is my Son! I love him! Listen to him, all of you!"

As the boat rocked from side to side, Jesus heard another sound. It wasn't God's voice calling from heaven, but the voices of people. Many, many, people. And they were calling Jesus' name.

"Jesus! Jesus, help us!" they cried. The voices grew from a whisper to a rumble to a loud roar until Jesus looked up from the boat. He could hardly believe his eyes.

Dozens, hundreds, thousands of people, crammed the beach, waving and shouting, not wanting to miss this chance to be with Jesus.

The ache in Jesus' heart melted, replaced with compassion for all the sick and sad people. "I'm coming!" he said, and rowed the boat quickly towards the shore, filled with love for the people who believed in him.

All afternoon, Jesus healed people. "I can walk again!" said one. "I can see for the first time!" cried another. Just hearing of God's love and kindness calmed the hearts of many in the crowd.

The sun rose high in the sky, shining golden light on the emerald-green hills. The hours rolled by, and the sky turned from brilliant blue to deep purple. The first stars blinked awake.

The disciples, who had been busy all day helping other people in the villages, finally found Jesus. The sight of the crowds amazed them.

"Jesus," said one. "We are so far from the villages. How will we feed all these people?"

"Perhaps you need to tell them to leave, so they can go find something to eat before dark," said another.

"No need for that," Jesus replied.

"But they're hungry!" said a disciple. "You must be hungry, too. You've been here all day long with nothing to eat."

"You feed them," Jesus said.

"What? Us?" The disciples looked at one another, then at Jesus. "We don't have the money to buy food for all these people! There must be over five thousand!"

"You feed them," Jesus repeated.

The disciples asked around to see if anyone had brought food. "Does anybody have food to share?" they asked hopefully.

"No," the people answered. "We didn't think to bring any, we were in such a hurry to find Jesus. What are we going to do? It's late and we are hungry!"

Andrew, one of the disciples, felt a tug on his sleeve. A little boy held up a basket. "I'll share," he said.

Andrew peeked inside the basket, then nodded. "Come with me," he said, then led him to Jesus. "Show him what you have," he told the boy, then said to Jesus, "This is all the food we could find."

Jesus lifted the cloth that covered the basket. Inside, five round loaves of bread nestled alongside two fish. "Perfect," he smiled.

"But Lord!" said Andrew. "Five loaves of bread and two fish will never feed this many people!"

Jesus ignored his words. "Everyone, sit down!" he called out to the crowds. "It's supper time!"

"Thank goodness!" the people muttered. "We're starving!" They gathered in groups and sat down. Voices hushed, and stomachs grumbled and growled.

Jesus held up the loaves of bread and the two fish towards heaven. "Thank you, Father, for this food," he prayed. "Bless everyone gathered here today. Amen."

He handed bread to each of the disciples. "Share it with the people," he said.

The disciples broke the bread and handed it out. "Take some, and pass it around."

One by one, people broke bread and gave it to neighbours, friends and even strangers. Soon, the air babbled with happy voices as empty bellies filled with food.

"Best bread ever," some said.

"The fish is delicious, too," said others.

"Have some more!"

"No thank you, I'm full."

A broad-faced moon climbed high into the indigo sky as the disciples passed baskets around to gather up the leftovers. Nobody could have imagined that there would be any food left, but there was. They collected twelve baskets of leftovers!

Mothers and fathers cradled sleeping children on their shoulders. "Let's go home," they said. Others spread out blankets and slept under the stars.

Nobody went to sleep hungry that night. Jesus had fed them all, not only with food, but also with God's love.

The Good Neighbour

Jesus loved to talk about God. He spoke to rich people and poor people and everyone in between. People did not always like what Jesus had to say, however, and often tried to trick him with questions.

This happened one day when Jesus met with a group of people who thought they already knew everything there was to know about God. One 'expert' asked him, "What do I have to do to be sure that I will live with God forever in heaven?"

The man wanted to test Jesus to see if he knew the Ten Commandments that had guided the people since Moses led them to the Promised Land centuries before.

Instead of giving the answer, Jesus asked the man a question. "What do our rules say?"

The man sneered. What an easy question – everybody knew the answer to that. It was the first of the commandments. "Love the Lord your God with all your heart, all your soul, all your strength, all your mind. And love your neighbour as you love yourself," he said.

"That's right!" Jesus said. "Follow that rule and you will enjoy a blessed and endless life with God, in this world and in heaven to come."

That should have been the end of the discussion, but then the man asked Jesus another question. "But who is my neighbour?"

"Let me tell you a story," Jesus answered. Jesus often explained things in parables, simple stories he used to teach God's truths using examples from everyday life.

The crowd around Jesus got very quiet. They all wanted to hear Jesus' story.

"There was a man," he said, "travelling on a road between the cities of Jericho and Jerusalem. Not very many people used this road. A couple of robbers crouched behind some large rocks, waiting for lonely travellers to pass by.

"'Aha!' the robbers thought when they saw the man walking past. 'Let's get him!'

"They pounced from behind the rocks where they were hiding, beat the man, took his money and even his clothes, and ran off, leaving him nearly dead.

"The poor man lay there, so hurt he was unable even to cry for help. The hot sun burned in the sky, and flies buzzed around him, but he could do nothing.

"In the distance, a priest walking the road saw what looked like a bundle lying in a ditch. He shielded his eyes from the sun, trying to figure out what it could be. He came just close enough to see that it was a badly hurt man, and then stopped in his tracks.

"'I wonder if he is dead or alive?' the priest thought, but he did not care enough to find out. 'It isn't my fault he's lying there,' he said to himself. He looked left and right to see if anyone was watching, then scurried away as fast as he could."

The people listening to Jesus did not say a word. Jesus continued.

"After awhile, another man, who worked in the temple, came down the road. He saw the injured man in the ditch. 'What in the world could that be?' he wondered, then quietly stepped over to take a closer look.

'A man!' he said, surprised. 'And he looks badly hurt. But what can I do? Someone else can help him, not me. I have other things to get on with.' He looked left and right and then hurried to the opposite side of the road and away from there, as fast as his legs could go.

"Next," Jesus said, "came a Samaritan, from the country of Samaria."

"A Samaritan!" grumbled the crowd. The Samaritans and the Jews hated each other, and had been enemies for hundreds of years. They knew that the Samaritan wouldn't help the poor man beaten by robbers.

"The Samaritan," Jesus said, "felt sorry for the injured man. He did not look left and right to see if anyone was watching. He did not scurry and hurry away. He bent down, and tenderly cleaned the man's wounds. He wrapped the man in bandages, gently placed him on his own donkey, and took him to the nearest inn.

"He stayed up all night taking care of the injured man, and did not sleep a wink.

"The next day, when it was time for him to be on his way, the Samaritan handed the innkeeper a large sum of money. 'Please take care of this man until he is well,' he said. 'I will stop by here the next time I am on this road, and if it has cost you anything more to help him, I will pay you back.'"

At this point in the parable, Jesus looked carefully at every person watching him. "Now," he said, turning to the man who had first asked the question. "Which one of the three men on the road acted like a good neighbour to the man who was beaten by robbers? Was it the priest? The temple worker? Or. . . the Samaritan?"

What would the so-called expert say? How would he answer Jesus' question?

"Humph!" the man said. He could not bring himself to say the word, 'Samaritan'. So he mumbled, "The neighbour was the man who showed mercy and kindness."

Jesus hid a smile. "You are absolutely right! Now you know the answer to your question. A neighbour is not just the person who lives next door. If you truly follow God, and want to live with God forever, you must be kind and helpful to everyone, including strangers, people who are different from you and even people you do not like. Go now, and do this."

The Last Supper

Many people followed Jesus and believed that he truly was God's Son. But others did not, especially the powerful religious leaders and rulers. They felt threatened by Jesus, and grew extremely angry. They decided that Jesus had to die.

Every year, the time when Moses led the people of Israel out of slavery in Egypt was remembered with a special celebration called Passover.

"Tonight, we will eat the Passover meal together," Jesus told his disciples. He knew that he was about to die and that it would be the last time he could eat this meal with his beloved disciples before he returned to his Father in heaven. There were so many things he needed to tell them.

The first few stars of the night twinkled sadly as the disciples trudged up the stairs to the room Jesus had chosen for this special meal.

The warm, golden bread smelled heavenly. A pitcher of sweet, red wine glittered in the candlelight.

Jesus picked up a loaf of bread and held it in his strong, yet gentle, hands. He blessed the bread and then broke the loaf in pieces and passed them to the disciples. "This is my body," he told them, "which will be broken for you."

Then he blessed the wine and filled their cups. "This is my blood, which is given for you. Whenever you eat this meal, with the bread and wine, remember me," he told them. They did not understand that he was talking about his death, but sat quietly, so that later, they could remember everything.

After they had eaten, Jesus took off his cloak and tied a servant's towel around his waist. One by one, he knelt down and washed his disciples' tired and dirty feet.

"What do you think that you are doing?" the disciple, Peter, asked when it came to his turn. "You are our teacher, and that is the job of a servant! You can't wash my feet!" But Jesus insisted.

Afterwards, he explained. "You call me Teacher and Lord, and I am. So if I serve you this way, you must do the same. No one person is better than another. If you believe in me, you will remember this, and take care of each other. This is the new commandment for all who follow me. Love each other as I love you."

Jesus sighed sadly, and said, "I know each of you so very well, and I know that one of you will betray me, and turn me over to those who will kill me."

"No!" said eleven of the disciples, horrified. But Judas, who had met secretly with the religious leaders who hated Jesus, had indeed agreed to betray Jesus. He quickly got up and left.

"There are still so many things I want to tell you," Jesus said to the remaining eleven disciples. "So much you need to know! I am going to die soon. I must do this to save people from sin, from the ways that people hurt one another and turn from God. But I will rise from the dead and return to my Father in heaven, and one day, you will join me there."

"But how?" they asked. "How will we find our way to heaven? We don't know how to get there!"

"My dear little children!" he said. "I know that your hearts are sad. But don't be troubled or afraid. I am the way to heaven. When your time comes, I will return, and take you to live there with me forever.

"After I am gone, I will send the Holy Spirit to you, to comfort and guide you. You will not be left alone. I will give you peace that the world will never be able to give you. So be at peace. Believe in God and believe in me."

"Oh no, Jesus, no!" the disciples cried. "You can't die! We can't bear it!"

"This is a very sad time, and there will be other sad times," Jesus said. "But when you are feeling sorrowful, remember that you won't feel that way forever. God's love is more powerful than anything in the world. You will find joy again. Trust me!"

Jesus took a deep breath. "But now it is my time to go. You are my friends, and I love you." He stood up from the table and with heavy steps, left the room, walking down the stairs and outside to a garden at the base of a hill, the Mount of Olives. All the disciples followed.

The branches of the olive trees hung heavy with leaves. A breeze rustled the leaves, which fell like tears on the garden path.

"Wait here, and pray for me," Jesus whispered to the disciples as he walked deeper into the garden. Clouds rolled across the sky, covering the stars in darkness. Jesus' heart felt as heavy as the stone that he knelt beside.

"Father!" he prayed, his heart nearly breaking. "Does the end have to happen this way? But I am yours, and I will do whatever you say."

Jesus returned to the disciples, and found them all curled up, asleep. They were tired inside and out, and could not stay awake to pray.

The sound of angry voices, stomping feet and clanging weapons interrupted them as a crowd of outraged soldiers and rulers and religious leaders stormed into the garden. Judas led the way, and when he saw Jesus, he ran over and kissed him on the cheek. This was the signal to the crowd to grab Jesus and arrest him.

Terrified, the disciples all ran away, afraid for their lives.

The guards dragged Jesus off, to a courtyard where all the leaders who hated Jesus waited to judge him.

"Who do you think you are?" the soldiers yelled at him. "You think you are the king of the Jews? Then wear this!" They jammed a crown made of sharp thorns onto his head.

"You say you are the son of God?" the religious leaders questioned, furious.

"I am the Son of God," said Jesus.

"You will die for this!" they shouted at him.

When Judas, who had betrayed Jesus, heard this, he regretted what he had done, but it was too late.

The soldiers made Jesus carry a heavy wooden cross through the city to a hillside. A crowd gathered to watch. Many people who believed in Jesus were there to see what would happen. But nobody tried to stop him from being killed, because everyone was afraid that the leaders might kill them, too.

The angry people nailed his hands and feet onto the cross, for that is how criminals died back then. They shouted and cursed him.

"If you're really the son of God, why doesn't he save you?" they jeered.

Jesus knew that he had to die on the cross to show the power of God's love. So he did not return the crowd's anger. Instead, he prayed. "Forgive them, Father. These people do not know what they are doing." For if they had believed that Jesus was the Son of God, they would never have dared to kill him.

Jesus' mother, Mary, her sister, and another woman watched nearby. Mary remembered all that she had kept in the pocket of her heart since her son's birth. She remembered that glorious night when the stars and angels sang and she had held her beautiful baby boy in her arms. Now, he was being held by the arms of the cross.

She remembered the joyful shepherds stumbling into the stable, eager to tell everyone, "This is God's Son!" Now, the shepherds' joyful voices were replaced by the cruel, angry words of the crowd.

She remembered the wise men who had travelled from so far away to bow down before the family and bring their treasures to her little child, the Messiah, God's chosen one.

She looked around at all the sneering faces of people who had come from all over to watch her son die. And she began to cry.

Jesus saw her. He saw his disciple, John, nearby. "Here is your son," he said to Mary, nodding his head towards John. "Here is your mother," he said to John. And from that day on, John took Mary into his home and cared for her.

Fierce storm clouds thundered across the sky, blocking out the light of the afternoon sun. All the beautiful colours of creation seemed to drain away. Jesus cried out, "Father God, my life belongs to you. Take my spirit into your loving hands!" And with those final words, Jesus died.

All of creation, all the beautiful world that God had created with such love and joy, shuddered with grief. The mountains trembled, the land shook, massive rocks split in two.

A rich man named Joseph, who loved and followed Jesus, asked permission to take Jesus' body so he could bury him properly. He wrapped him in a clean linen cloth, like Mary had wrapped her baby in strips of cloth after his birth. But instead of a manger-cradle, this time Jesus was placed inside a large cave, which was used as a grave.

Normally, they would have done more to prepare his body for burial, but the Sabbath was about to begin, and it was forbidden to do any work during this holy time. So Joseph rolled a huge, heavy stone over the doorway, to keep the body safe.

The day Jesus died was the saddest day heaven and earth had ever known. It seemed that the light of the world had gone out, for it had.

It seemed like the end.

But it was not, for God had other plans.

The First Easter

Mary Magdalene paced back and forth, alone in her quiet home. She still could not believe what had happened. Some months ago, Jesus had healed her from a terrible illness, and she had followed him ever since. She believed him to be God's Son and the Saviour of the world. But now, he was dead.

The day before, Jesus had died in a terrible, terrible way, his lifeless body then placed in a tomb by another follower, Joseph. There had been no time to prepare it properly for burial. The Jewish laws prohibited any kind of work being done on the Sabbath, and Jesus died just as the Sabbath began. Mary would have to wait until the Sabbath ended, now only a few hours away.

Would this sad, awful day never end?

She passed the time in prayer and in sorrow. When the sun set and the endless day finally ended, Mary fell into a restless, dreamless sleep.

Wake up, Mary! A voice inside her startled her awake. Morning had arrived!

She hurried to prepare the spices and ointments to wash Jesus' body before his final burial. Then Mary stepped from her home into the darkness of the dawn. Waiting

for her in the shadows were several other women who, like Mary, had followed Jesus. Gentle fingers of light reached through the mist and fog and lit their way along the twisting path. Baby birds, tucked into their night-time nests, stretched their wings and beaks and chirped and peeped as if to say, "Good morning!"

It felt like anything but a good morning to the women as they crept quietly towards the tomb, their steps heavy with grief. Their lives would never be the same now that Jesus was gone. "Will there ever be joy in the world again?" they wondered.

They were sad, sad, sad. Sad beyond words sad.

"How are we going to move that heavy stone that blocks the doorway to the cave where Jesus is?" asked one of the women. "We will never be able to do that by ourselves."

But as they neared the cave, the earth began to shimmy and shake, then rumble and roar. An earthquake! As the earth trembled, they ran as quickly as they could and came to the place where Jesus' body had been taken after his death.

And there, sitting on top of the stone that had been rolled away from the door sat an angel! The angel dazzled like lightning, and wore magnificent robes whiter than the whitest white.

The earth stopped shaking, but not the women. They dropped their jars of spices, fell to the ground at the angel's feet, and covered their heads with their hands.

"Do not be afraid," the angel said. *Do not be afraid.* These were the same words the angel had said to Mary when she learned she would give birth to Jesus, and to Joseph when he didn't understand, and to the shepherds when they were told the good news of Jesus' birth. *Do not be afraid.*

The women sat up so they could listen more carefully.

"Why are you here looking for Jesus in a graveyard?" the angel asked. "This is a place for those who are dead. But I bring you good news – great news – the best news in the whole world! Jesus is not dead. Jesus is alive! ALIVE!"

Alive? How could that be? The women could not believe their ears. They had seen Jesus on the cross, and seen him take his last breath, had seen his lifeless body carried to this cave. Alive? Impossible!

"See for yourselves," the angel smiled. "Go in and take a look."

They got up and hurried into the cave and found it just as the angel said. All they saw was a pile of neatly folded cloths, the ones that had wrapped the body of Jesus, which was nowhere to be found. Where could he be?

"Remember?" the angel said. "Before Jesus died? He told you he would rise from the dead. Everything has happened as he said it would, as God planned all along. God is more powerful than death! Now it is your job to tell the disciples what you have found. Everyone must hear the good news of Jesus' resurrection. Run! Go! Tell! Jesus is alive!"

The women's feet did not feel heavy any more, but light as air. *Hurry! Hurry! Hurry! Good news to share! Everyone must hear!*

Oh, glorious day! What had begun as the saddest day in the world had suddenly become the most joyful day in all creation. For as the sun rose that glorious Easter morning, so did the Son of God. Jesus rose from the dead, never to die again! The sun shone brighter than ever before, the sky a brilliant blue. The birds burst forth in song. The trees waved their branches as if clapping hands with glee.

By the time Mary and the women arrived back in town, they were breathless. Still, Mary climbed the stairs two at a time, reaching the place where the disciples had eaten that last supper with Jesus only a short time before. She burst inside and found the windows shut and the disciples huddled together in the darkness.

"Wake up! Wake up!" Mary shouted. "I have good news! Great news! The best news in the whole world! Jesus is alive!"

"Wh-wh-what?" the disciples said. "That's ridiculous! We don't believe you."

"It's true," Mary said. "I saw it with my own eyes. The cave is empty. Jesus is alive! He told us this would happen, and it has."

"Nonsense," said the disciples. Mary could not convince them otherwise. Finally, she left.

The disciples stayed in the dark room all day. That night, as they cooked fish for dinner and talked with one another about Jesus, a special visitor appeared out of nowhere.

"Peace be with you," the visitor said, standing there among them.

It sounded like Jesus – but how could that be?

"It's a ghost!" they shouted, terrified.

"Why are you afraid?" the visitor asked. "It's me, Jesus. Go ahead; touch my hands, my feet. Does a ghost have flesh and bones like this?"

The last time they had seen Jesus, he had just died an awful death. Now, he was healthy and whole, shining with a light that did not come from the candles in the room, but from deep within Jesus himself.

"How can it be you?" they asked.

Again, Jesus said, "Peace be with you. God loves you all so much that he sent me, his only Son, to die on the cross to save you from sin, from everything that tries to separate you from God. If you believe in me, you believe in God, who forgives you for all the ways you turn away from him.

"Now, I am sending you to share this good news with others. I am alive! Death cannot stop me, God's love is forever."

Then Jesus breathed on them and said, "I give you the Holy Spirit, which is the very breath of God. You cannot see the Spirit, but the Spirit gives you life. When you are sad, the Spirit will comfort you. When you feel lost, the Spirit will guide you."

And then he left them.

The disciples believed, and a rush of joy beyond anything they had ever experienced filled them to overflowing.

They could hardly wait to tell others the good news!

Breakfast on the Beach

A few weeks after Jesus had died and risen from the dead, several of the disciples, including Peter and John, met by the Sea of Galilee at night.

"I'm going fishing," Peter said. He'd been a fisherman before he began to follow Jesus, and he loved to fish. He didn't know what else to do, now that Jesus wasn't with them in the way he had been before.

"We'll go with you," the others said.

They fished and fished all night, but caught nothing.

The sun started to rise over the water, which glimmered with golden light. Gentle waves lapped the side of the fishing boat.

On the beach, in the shadows, the disciples saw the figure of a man. "Fellows!" the man called out to them. "Catch anything?"

"No," they answered, discouragement in their voices.

"Throw your nets on the other side of the boat, and you'll catch some fish!" the man replied.

What did they have to lose? They did as the man said.

Silver-scaled fish wriggled and wiggled in great heaps and the nets grew heavy with them, so that the disciples could not pull them into the boat.

The early morning shadows lifted and John saw the face of the man on the beach. His heart leapt in his chest.

"It's Jesus!" he shouted. "The Lord!"

Peter, still in the boat, dove headfirst into the water, his arms and legs thrashing and splashing in his hurry to get to Jesus. The others followed in the boat, dragging the nets of fish to shore.

A charcoal fire crackled nearby. The delicious smell of grilled fish and fresh bread greeted the disciples. "Breakfast time!" Jesus smiled. "Who's hungry?"

The men were starving not only for breakfast, but for a little more time with their beloved Jesus. He filled their plates with food and passed them around. They remembered that last supper, when Jesus said, "When you break bread together, remember me." How could they forget, with Jesus right there in the midst of them?

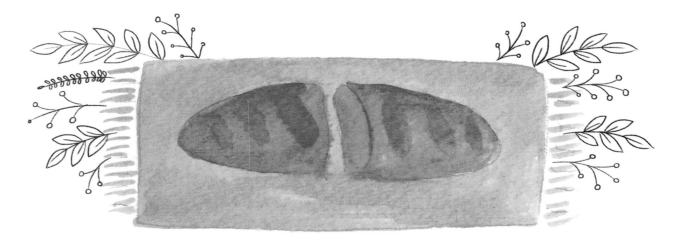

The tired and happy disciples ate every last bite of the food Jesus had cooked for them. Breakfast had never tasted so good! Then they stretched out in the warm sand to rest.

Jesus and Peter walked together, their feet leaving prints in the wet sand. When they were some way away from the rest of the disciples, Jesus spoke.

"Peter," he said, nodding his head towards the disciples. "Do you love me?"

Peter gulped. What kind of question was this? "Of course, you know that I do," he said.

"Feed my lambs," Jesus said.

Then Jesus asked him again.

"Peter, do you love me more than anyone? Do you love me as you love God?"

"Yes, Lord!" Peter said a second time. "You already know that."

"Feed my sheep," Jesus said.

A third time, Jesus asked, "Peter, do you love me even more than life?"

Peter's face fell. How could Jesus keep asking him the same question over and over again? Didn't Jesus believe him when he said, "I love you"?

"You know everything!" Peter cried. "You know that I love you. I love you with all my heart and soul and mind and strength."

"Feed my sheep," Jesus answered.

Peter remembered that Jesus had once called himself the Good Shepherd, and referred to his followers as sheep. Then Peter understood that Jesus wanted him to take care of other people who would one day follow Jesus.

Jesus explained further. "It won't always be easy to live as I have taught you. People won't always understand. But even when it is difficult to follow me, I need you to keep trying. Be kind to others in my name. Forgive each other. Tell everyone in the whole wide world about me! I will give life to those who believe in me. And most of all, remember this: I am with you, forever and always. Even when you cannot see me, I am close by. I am never far away."

Peter promised himself that he would do his very best to follow Jesus, to take care of his sheep.

He kept that promise.

Jesus appeared to his disciples several more times in different places. Then, he gathered them together one last time. "It is time for me to return to my Father in heaven. I will see you there one day. For now, I command you to go out into all parts of the world and teach people about me, about God's love and forgiveness. Remember everything that I have taught you. And never forget that I am with you forever, until the end of time."

Now, Jesus did many other wonderful things, and still does, to this very day. If the world were filled with books in stacks as high as mountains, they could not contain all the glorious stories of Jesus, the Son of God.

Read these stories in your Bible...

The Old Testament

The Creation	Genesis 1
The Garden of Eden	Genesis 2–3
Noah and the Ark	Genesis 6–9
A Son Named Laughter	Genesis 12–21
Joseph and his Amazing Coat	Genesis 30; 37, 30
The Baby in the Basket	Exodus 1–4
The Ten Plagues of Egypt	Exodus 4–23
David and Goliath	Samuel 1
Jonah and the Big Fish	Jonah

The New Testament

Jesus is Born	Luke 1; Matthew 1
The Sermon on the Mount	Matthew 5–7
Four Faithful Friends	Matthew 9; Mark 2; Luke 5
Jesus Feeds Five Thousand People	Matthew 14; Mark 6; Luke 9; James 6
The Good Neighbour	Luke 10
The Last Supper	Matthew 26–27; Mark 14–15; Luke 22:–23; James 13–19
The First Easter	Matthew 27–28; Mark 16; Luke 24: James 20–21
Breakfast on the Beach	John 21